HORSES

GROOVY TUBE BOOK

FACT BOOK • ANIMALS • GAME BOARD

Written by Susan Ring
For Chelsea Dowling, for all her help, her friendship, and her love of horses

Illustrated by Ruth Palmer
With love and thanks to Kate and Geoff

Conceived, developed, and designed by the creative team at innovativeKids®.
Game by innovativeKids®
Patent #'s 6,079,748; 6,247,729
Copyright © 2006 by innovativeKids®
All rights reserved
Published by innovativeKids®, a division of innovative USA®, Inc.
18 Ann Street, Norwalk, CT 06854
iKids is a registered trademark in Canada and Australia.
ISBN: 978-1-58476-409-0
Not for individual sale
10 9 8 7

Special thanks to Dr. Jenifer Nadeau, an equine extension specialist and assistant professor at the University of Connecticut, for fact checking this book.

PHOTO CREDITS
Cover: MIMOTITO/Digital Vision/Getty Images; p. 4: Digital Vision/Getty Images; p. 5: Sami Sarkis/Photodisc Blue/Getty Images; p. 6: © Juniors Bildarchiv/Alamy; p. 7: Photodisc Collection/Photodisc Blue/Getty Images; p. 8: © Alaska Stock LLC/Alamy; p. 13: © Lankowsky/Alamy; p. 17: Tom Buchta; p. 21: © Chris Warham/Alamy

The First Horses

For thousands of years, horses have been helping people—by pulling equipment, carrying items while traveling, and providing transportation.

But before they began helping people, early relatives of today's horses roamed the fields of North America and Asia. Horses, also called equines (EE-kwines), have lived on Earth for about 55 million years! Today, there are about 150 different breeds throughout the world.

Did you know that horses didn't always look the way they do now? Fossils show that horses were once as small as foxes. And they had several hoofed toes on their feet! Over millions of years, horses developed long legs to help them travel great distances, long necks for grazing, and a single toe in the form of a hoof.

Arabian

Cave painting

The Arabian is the oldest purebred horse, dating back more than 2,000 years.

Horses didn't always have a home in the United States. Settlers from Spain, called Spaniards, brought the first horses to the United States in the 1500s.

Horses have been inspiring artists and writers for thousands of years. In Spain and France, horses appear in cave paintings that are more than 15,000 years old. Scientists believe the cave paintings are an example of how important horses were to people, even long ago.

Andalusians were once used in battles and ridden by knights.

Andalusian

3

All in the Family

Not all horses are equal . . . but they're all equidae (EH-kwih-day). Equidae is the name of the scientific family horses belong to. Horses aren't the only animals in this family—donkeys and zebras are equidae, too.

Zebras live in Africa and graze on the grasslands. They all are white with black stripes. Or are they black with white stripes? Some scientists think that zebras have stripes to confuse their enemies when they gather together in large groups, called herds. Others believe the stripes help zebras blend in with their surroundings. Either way, zebras are able to tell each other apart. And they take very good care of each other. If one member of the herd gets lost, they will all go and look for it. Each herd stays together for life.

Believe it or not, every zebra has a different stripe pattern!

Donkeys are also relatives of horses. They are strong animals that can carry heavy loads over long distances. People all around the world depend on donkeys to help them travel and work. They are also popular pets.

Donkeys' eyes, ears, and brains are larger than those of horses, and their feet can withstand walking around on rough ground without wearing horseshoes—or donkeyshoes. Like horses and zebras, donkeys like to have company and prefer to live in large groups.

One type of zebra, called the quagga (KWA-guh), roamed the African plains until it became extinct in the late 1800s. Its hair was a yellowish color, and it had black and white stripes only on its head and neck.

5

Baby Horses

When springtime arrives so do baby horses! Almost all baby horses, called foals, are born in the spring when there is fresh green grass on the ground and plenty of water to drink. This ensures that the foals will have plenty to eat and drink to help them become healthy adults.

Shetland Pony

Most mares have just one baby at a time. They carry their babies for about 11 months before the foals are born.

Adult female horses are called mares, and adult males are called stallions. A female foal is called a filly, and a male foal is called a colt. A horse is considered to be fully grown when it is about three or four years old. Horses can live to be 20 to 30 years old. A horse's age can be estimated by looking at its front teeth. An older horse's teeth are more worn down and longer.

Can you imagine being born with legs as long as a grown-up's? When foals are born, they have such long legs that their mouths can barely reach down to the ground to eat grass!

Just minutes after being born, a foal is able to stand on its own. Within an hour after the foal is born, it can walk, and after just one day, it can run alongside its mom. In the wild, this helps the baby keep up with its mother and run away from danger. In just a few weeks, the foal will be grazing and eating other solid foods.

7

Horse Sense

Horses have keen senses that help them survive and defend themselves in the wild.

Hearing

Horses have excellent hearing and can hear sounds that people cannot. Their ears have 10 pairs of muscles that help them move their ears in almost any direction. This comes in handy when a horse is bending down to eat or drink and when a horse wants to listen for an enemy sneaking up behind it. But beware—when a horse puts its ears back, it means it is afraid or angry. If its ears are forward, it means the horse is curious.

Sight

Horses have very large eyes placed on the sides of their heads. This allows them to see what is around them and helps keep them safe in open areas.

Smell

Horses also depend on their sense of smell. When a horse really wants to smell something, it might curl back its top lip to pick up even more of a scent.

Touch

Another sense that horses rely on is their sense of touch. Horses like to nibble, nuzzle, and nudge each other. This is one way they communicate and form close bonds. They also communicate with each other through whinnies, snorts, squeals, and grunts.

When horses feel threatened, they might kick, rear up on their back legs, or bite to defend themselves, but their first instinct is to run away from danger.

As animals of prey, horses need to stay alert for danger. Instead of sleeping all through the night, horses take several naps each day, usually while standing up. A horse's legs "lock" so it can sleep standing up without falling over.

Can you imagine knowing which group of friends is yours by its smell? Each herd of horses has its own group smell, which helps it stay together. A foal will recognize its mother by her smell, as well.

Horses are incredibly strong, but in the wild they are prey and are sometimes chased down by hungry predators, such as mountain lions and coyotes.

Mustangs

Horse of a Different Color

What in blazes is a blaze? Besides its coloring, a horse may have markings on its head or legs.

Blaze
A wide white marking down a horse's face

Stripe
A thin white marking down a horse's face

Star
A white shape, sometimes in the form of a star, on a horse's forehead

Snip
A small patch of white hair near a horse's nose

Sock
White hair on the lower part of a horse's leg

Stocking
A longer section of white hair on a horse's leg from hoof to knee

Appaloosa

Palomino

Horses come in many different colors and color combinations. Some horses are all one color, such as brown, black, or gray. Other horses have large patches of color, and some have small spots.

 Chestnut: reddish-brown color

 Dun: tan color, with a black stripe down the back

Bay: tan to reddish brown, with a black mane and tail, and black lower legs

Palomino: a golden-colored coat with a white mane and tail

Skewbald: large white and brown patches

Piebald: large patches of white and black

 Spotted: coat with small to medium-sized spots

 Flea-bitten: gray coat with tiny black or brown specks

Dapple gray: gray coat with lighter-colored spots or patches

Roan: reddish-brown to black horse with white hairs flecked on a different colored coat, creating the colors blue, red, or strawberry

Friesian

On Your High Horse

How do you measure a horse? Instead of using inches or millimeters, a horse is measured in hands. This form of measurement actually comes from using a man's hand to measure how high a horse stands.

But not every man's hand is the same size, so people decided to make one hand equal to 4 inches. But it's still called a hand.

When is a horse not a horse? A horse has to be 14.2 hands high (hh) to be considered a horse. Shires, Belgians, and Clydesdales are three of the tallest horse breeds and often are 18 hh.

Belgian

Falabella

Horses that are under 14 hh are called ponies. Shetland ponies are strong, gentle animals that are often kept as pets.

The smallest horses are Falabellas. They are about 7.5 hh. They are called miniature horses. Some Falabellas are used as guide horses for visually impaired people.

Just like you have to take off your shoes when you get measured, so does a horse. An accurate measurement is from the ground up to a horse's shoulder. The withers is the highest point on the horse's shoulder, so that's where you stop measuring.

Withers (Approximately 17 hh)

Clydesdale

Black Beauty, a miniature horse that stands 18.5 inches tall, is the smallest horse on record. The tallest horse on record was a Shire named Sampson. He was 7 ft. 2 in. (21.5 hh)!

Out West

It's hard to imagine a cowboy without a horse. Back in the days of the Wild West, horses helped cowboys travel and move cattle across miles of land. Before huge cattle ranches were fenced in, a cowboy's job was to drive, or move, cattle to grazing areas and to protect them from wild animals and thieves. Horses carried cowboys over rugged mountains, across rivers and streams, and through all kinds of harsh weather.

Native Americans also depended on horses for hunting and traveling. They often rode Appaloosas and pintos.

Pinto

Today, cowboys continue to rely on their horses for help. Most ranch horses today are Quarter Horses. The Quarter Horse is the oldest horse breed in America. It got its name because it was bred to race short distances, no further than a quarter of a mile.

Cowboys use a Western type of saddle. This is a saddle with a horn on it. Even though it's handy to grab on to, the horn is actually used to hold a cowboy's lasso. The lasso is usually used to rope in cattle.

PONY EXPRESS

How did people get their mail in 1860? It was delivered by riders on horseback who worked for the Pony Express. It was actually a dangerous and very difficult job for riders, who carried the mail 2,000 miles across the country.

Quarter Horses

Wild Horses

Not all horses have an owner, a barn, or even someone to ride them. Some horses still run wild in different parts of the world. Spanish settlers brought horses to the United States in the 1500s. Many of their horses ran off and began to survive in the wild.

Descendants of these horses are still roaming free today as feral horses. Some of these horses, called Mustangs, live on the western scrubland of the United States. Like all horses, they run in large herds. The horses are strong and powerful and live through harsh, cold winters. Because they run over rocky land in the West, their feet have developed a special shape to protect them from getting hurt. Some Mustangs even have blue eyes!

Only one type of horse is really a true wild horse. It is the Asiatic wild horse —which is easier to say than its other name, Przewalski's (shuh-VAL-skeez) horse. These small horses are extinct in their natural habitat in Mongolia, which is part of eastern Asia, but they have been bred in zoos and reintroduced to the wild.

"Saltwater cowboys" round them up and have them swim across the channel to the mainland. It's about a 10-minute swim. Once the ponies reach shore, people buy them to keep as pets.

Wild horses also live in the eastern part of the United States. Ponies run free on Assateague Island, off the coast of Virginia and Maryland. In order to control the herd populations, every year the ponies take a nice swim!

Mustang

The word mustang comes from a Spanish word that means "stray."

And They're Off!

A horse's body is built for running. It has long, powerful legs, strong muscles, and lightweight bones. Add to this a horse's large lungs and heart, and a horse has no problem traveling long distances at great speeds.

Some horses are bred especially for their speed and stamina. Many become racehorses. The most popular breed of racehorse in the world is the Thoroughbred.

Thoroughbred

Thoroughbreds often begin their racing careers at just two years old. Some racehorses have even become famous celebrities! One racehorse, Seabiscuit, had a movie made about his life.

Most Thoroughbreds are a solid color, such as black or brown, and their necks are longer than most horses. Their hearts are more than 8 times as heavy as a person's heart, and their large nostrils allow them to take in plenty of air while running. It's no wonder they are the fastest of all breeds!

Polo is the fastest game played on horseback. It was first played by men and women in Asia over 2,000 years ago. Today, Argentina is known for its great players and polo ponies.

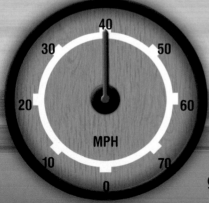

Horses move at different speeds called gaits. A trot is a bit faster than walking. Horses trot at about 7 to 10 miles per hour. When they want to speed up, horses canter. A canter is about 10 to 15 miles per hour. When they really get going, horses gallop at speeds starting at 20 to 25 miles per hour. Some horses can gallop up to almost 40 miles per hour!

Horse Power

People use the term horsepower to describe an engine's power. This term actually comes from measuring the energy a workhorse uses when pulling an object. Workhorses are also known as draft horses. They are large, strong breeds that can pull wagons and carts that weigh several tons. In fact, elephants are the only land animals that are stronger than horses.

Workhorses are usually 16 to 20 hh and are the tallest of the horse breeds. They can also weigh more than a ton—that's more than 2,000 pounds!

Did you know that some horses have feathers? The Percheron, one of the most popular breeds of workhorse, has long hair—called feathers—on its legs, close to its feet. Other workhorses such as Shires and Clydesdales also have these feathers. Belgians usually do not have these feathers.

Percheron

Whether they're working, playing, or running, horses use a lot of energy. That's why they spend most of their time eating. A horse can graze for 16 hours a day! A horse's digestive tract is 100 feet long, allowing it to eat . . . and eat . . . and eat.

The Suffolk Punch is one of the oldest kinds of workhorses. These horses are usually a reddish color, and unlike other heavy breeds, they don't have feathers on their legs. They are not as large as some other draft horses and do not need to eat as much food as other heavy breeds.

Shire

Suffolk Punch

Today, tractors have replaced most workhorses on farms. But the engines in tractors are measured in horsepower!

Come Ride with Me

Do you know how to take care of a horse? Horses have lots of likes and dislikes. They don't like being chased or tied up so tightly that they can't move their heads. They do like to keep a routine.

Horses are herbivores, or plant eaters. They can't eat a lot at one time, so they like to spend hours nibbling, or grazing, on grass as they roam around a pasture. They also need hay and healthy grains, such as oats, barley, and corn. For treats, most horses like carrots, apples, or even peppermints.

Horses also need to be groomed, which means taking care of their coats. There are different kinds of tools that pick out dirt, remove sweat, and smooth their hair.

Hanoverian

Lipizzaners, Hanoverians, and Andalusians are a few of the popular breeds used in equine competitions.

English Saddle

Stirrup

One of the most exciting parts of taking care of a horse is riding it! Healthy horses need plenty of exercise. The key pieces of equipment you'll need for riding are:

Bridle - the leather headpiece that fits over the horse's head

Bit - goes in the horse's mouth so it can feel which direction it is being steered

Reins - held by the rider, they help steer the horse

Saddle - fastens around the horse's belly and is where the rider sits

There are many different ways to ride a horse. Some people ride on trails, while others jump over hurdles. There is also barrel racing, long-distance riding, and equine competition. Many people enjoy a competition called dressage, which tests horse and rider in obedience and teamwork.

Bridle

Bit

Reins

Lipizzaner

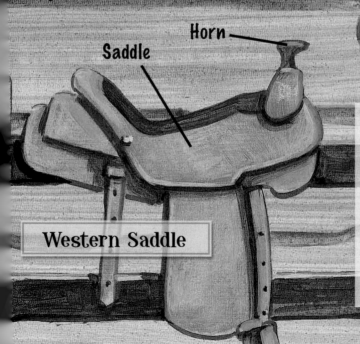

Horn

Saddle

Western Saddle

Watching a horse gallop or having a horse nuzzle up to you makes it easy to understand why these creatures have been loved for centuries. By returning love, care, and respect, a person can ensure that a horse will be a great companion—and the beautiful, strong, powerful creature it was born to be.

Questions

1. Who brought the first horses to the United States?

2. Spell the scientific name of the horse family.

3. Zebras live on which continent?

4. Describe a blaze.

5. Every zebra has a different stripe pattern. True or False?

6. Most horses are born in which season?

7. What is one major difference between English and Western saddles?

8. What can a newborn foal do within an hour after it's born?

9. What do Appaloosa, flea-bitten, and dapple gray horses have in common?

10. What is a female foal called?

11. What is a male foal called?

12. A horse is fully grown when it is how old?

13. Are horses predators or prey?

14. Horses are able to sleep soundly for 8 to 10 hours a night. True or False?

15. Which have better hearing—people or horses?

16. Where does a horse place its ears when it is afraid or angry?

17. What is a unique physical feature of some Mustangs?

18. If a horse is curious, what does it do with its ears?

19. A group of horses is called a: A) stampede B) herd C) pride

20. What is another term for a workhorse?

21. What will a horse do with its lips when it really wants to smell something?

22. How do horses communicate with other horses?

23. A horse's brain is smaller than a donkey's. True or False?

24. Name four different colors for horses.

25. Which is the world's most popular breed of racehorse? A) Friesian B) Thoroughbred C) Hanoverian

26. What color horse is usually a tan color with a black stripe down its back?

27. A horse can gallop about how fast?

28. What is the name of the horse pattern that has white hairs on a colored coat to create the colors blue, red, or strawberry?

29. Fossils show that ancient horses were once the size of which small animal?

30. A snip is on which part of a horse's body?

31. A skewbald horse is one that has not been tamed. True or False?

32. What color is a horse's sock or stocking?

33. A horse is measured in what type of units?

34. Which part of a horse's body is its withers?

35. A hand is equal to: A) 4 inches B) 1 foot C) 2 meters

36. Name a type of pony that is kept as a pet.

37. What is the smallest breed of horse?

38. What do some miniature horses do to help people?

39. What was the job of cowboys in the Wild West?

40. What breeds of horses were popular with Native Americans?